Quill It Easy

edited by **Tanya Fox**

Annie's Attic

Contents

Quill It Easy

Copyright © 2009 House of White Birches, Berne, Indiana 46711

EDITOR Tanya Fox

MANAGING EDITOR Barb Sprunger

ART DIRECTOR Brad Snow

PUBLISHING SERVICES DIRECTOR Brenda Gallmeyer

ASSISTANT ART DIRECTOR Nick Pierce

COPY SUPERVISOR Michelle Beck

COPY EDITORS Amanda Ladig, Susanna Tobias

TECHNICAL EDITOR Läna Schurb

PHOTOGRAPHY SUPERVISOR Tammy Christian

PHOTOGRAPHY Matt Owen

PHOTOGRAPHY STYLIST Tammy Steiner

GRAPHIC ARTS SUPERVISOR Ronda Bechinski

GRAPHIC ARTISTS Pam Gregory, Erin Augsburger

PRODUCTION ASSISTANTS Marj Morgan, Judy Neuenschwander

TECHNICAL ARTIST Nicole Gage

Printed in the United States of America
First Printing: 2009
ISBN: 978-1-59635-236-0

1 2 3 4 5 6 7 8 9

In recent years, a renewed interest in the age-old art of quilling has developed among paper crafters and card makers alike. Quilling is an inexpensive and practical way to add dimension to surfaces such as picture frames, lampshades, gift bags and tags, paper ornaments and handmade greeting cards.

What starts as a basic piece is transformed into a beautiful work of art covered with delicate coils and swirls of paper. Quilling requires only a few basic tools and thin strips of paper that can be purchased or easily made from your own paper stash, attributes that make it a craft that can be enjoyed even with the smallest of budgets.

What appears to be intensely detailed work is actually a very relaxing and tranquil art. Spending some time creating delicate quilled pieces at the end of a hectic day is a nice way to unwind. The added benefit of crafting one-of-a-kind cards and decorative pieces for your home or to give as gifts is priceless. You'll feel a real sense of accomplishment, and at the same time, you'll advance your crafting skills to a new level.

To get you started on your way to crafting beautiful quilled projects, we've provided an informative introduction to the art of quilling as well as a helpful shape gallery. The gallery shows samples of all the quilled shapes used for the projects we've included along with a brief description of how each shape is created.

Now, take a little time to familiarize yourself with the basic quilling shapes and get comfortable with the tools you'll be using. In no time at all, you'll be creating one-of-a-kind cards and gifts just like the ones in this book!

Happy crafting,

A special thanks goes to Delaware artist Ann Martin for providing the Quilling Basics and creating all the pieces for our Shape Gallery. Ann has been working with rolled-paper filigree since 2002 and has developed an inventive approach to designs and a precision of technique. Her quillwork has been featured in numerous paper-art and jewelry publications and a solo exhibition at the Brandywine River Museum in Pennsylvania, and she was filmed for the HGTV program "That's Clever". She conducts workshops and demonstrations and is a member of the North American Quilling Guild and Delaware by Hand, an organization linking artisans within the state of Delaware.

Quilling Basics

By **Ann Martin**

The age-old art of quilling is not as complicated as it appears at first glance, and it can be mastered by anyone with a bit of patience and a steady hand. It is one of the least expensive hobbies since it requires only a few simple materials, which you may already have at home.

Getting Started

Brand-new to quilling? Purchase a multicolor pack of quilling paper, or cut your own strips using computer text-weight paper and a paper cutter—they will be fine for practice. You will also need a tool with which to roll the paper strips.

Some quillers use only their fingers, but there is also the choice of a needle tool or slotted tool.

These can be purchased at arts and crafts stores or online, but it's easy to make your own tool by inserting a standard sewing needle into a bottle cork; the cork provides a comfortable handle.

If you like the security of a slot to help grab the end of the paper strip, make a slotted tool: Wearing goggles to protect your eyes, snip the tip off the eye end of a sewing needle, leaving the slot exposed. Using pliers, insert the needle point into the cork.

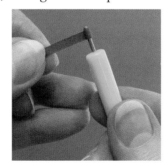

To use the slotted tool, slide the end of the paper strip into the slot. Referring to the instructions for the desired quilled motif in the Shape Gallery, page 5, turn the tool as directed with one hand as you guide the paper strip with the other.

Depending on the shape, you may apply a tiny amount of glue to the end with a toothpick and hold it in place for a few moments to dry. *Tip: Tear the end of the paper strip that will be glued rather than cutting it with scissors—it will blend smoothly, and the joining will be less noticeable.*

If you prefer that your coils not have the center crimp that a slotted tool produces, you will need to purchase or make a needle tool. Some quillers like to use an old-fashioned hat pin, corsage pin or even a cake tester as a needle tool.

It takes a little more effort to learn to quill with a needle tool, but with practice, you'll soon be producing an evenly rolled coil with a tiny, round center.

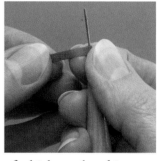

To begin, dampen your fingertips or the end of the paper strip and curve it across the tip of the needle. Using the thumb and index finger of whichever hand is most comfortable for you, roll the paper around the needle using relaxed, even pressure.

With practice, you'll find that your rolling tension becomes even and your shapes will be nearly identical in size.

Quilled Shape Gallery

By **Ann Martin**

Scrolls

Loose (Open) Scroll
Roll one end of strip, allowing the other end to curve gracefully.

C Scroll
Roll each end of strip toward center; the midsection will curve gracefully.

S Scroll
Visualize or lightly mark the midpoint of strip. Roll one end toward center; turn strip over and roll opposite end toward center.

V Scroll
Fold strip in half and roll each end outward.

Heart Scroll
Fold strip in half and roll each end inward toward midpoint.

Coils

Tight Coil
Roll strip on tool and adhere end in place without allowing coil to relax. Slide coil off tool.

Tight Coil Variations

Grape Roll
Form a Tight Coil and gently push up from underside of coil with the ball of a glass-head pin. Apply a thin coat of glue inside dome to hold rounded shape.

Oval Tight Coil
Form a Tight Coil; pinch gently with tweezers to form oval shape.

Sculptured Tight Coil
Form a Tight Coil and gently push up from underside with tip of quilling tool or pointed object, like a pen or orangewood stick. Apply a thin coat of glue inside coil to hold shape.

Relaxed Coils

Loose (Closed) Coil
Roll one end of strip and slide coil off tool. Tighten coil or allow it to relax to create coil of desired size; adhere outer end to outer edge.

Teardrop
Form a Loose (Closed) Coil. Pinch the join spot to create a point.

Shaped Teardrop
Form Teardrop; curve pointed end.

Marquise
Form a Loose (Closed) Coil. Pinch opposite sides to create two points, taking care to keep coil center positioned in center of Marquise.

Shaped Marquise
Grasp pointed ends of Marquise; curve one end upward and the other end downward.

Additional Relaxed Coils

Bunny Ears Coil
Form a Loose (Closed) Coil. Pinch two points fairly close to each other. Use tip of tool to indent curve between points.

Bunny Ears with Pointed Tip

Form a Bunny Ears Coil. Pinch bottom of curve.

Crescent

Form a Teardrop. Pinch a second point not directly opposite the first, and bend points toward each other.

Diamond

Form a Marquise. Pinch each side midway between first two points, but pinch less deeply than the first two points.

Rectangle

Form a Marquise. Turn the Marquise 45 degrees and pinch two additional points on opposite sides.

Semicircle

Form a Loose (Closed) Coil. Place coil on edge on flat surface and push down to form a flat side. Pinch coil at each end of flat area.

Triangle

Form a Loose (Closed) Coil; pinch three points.

Ring Coil

Use a cylindrical object to form a ring of desired size—for example, the handle of a quilling tool or glue stick. Wrap strip around the object several times; adhere end and slide coil off object. It may be helpful to apply a light coat of glue while wrapping.

Flowers

Basic Fringed Flower

A Fringed Flower can be made with a strip of almost any width and length. A standard size strip would be ⅜ x 3 inches. Use detail scissors to make fine, side-by-side cuts across width of strip. Snip as far

into the strip as possible without cutting all the way through. If you accidentally cut through the strip, adhere the ends together at the break and continue.

Roll fringed strip in the same manner as a Tight Coil. Adhere end, remove from tool, and fluff fringe open. To give the flower a natural look, use blade of scissors to curve fringe downward, as if curling paper ribbon.

Fringed Flower with Tight Coil Center

Fringe strip as for Basic Fringed Flower. Adhere a 3-inch strip of ⅛-inch-wide quilling paper to end of fringed strip. When glue is completely dry, insert narrow strip into quilling tool slot and roll until you reach the end of the fringed strip; adhere end.

Slide flower off tool and fluff fringe open, revealing the inner Tight Coil. The coil may remain flat or can be shaped into a dome or point.

Fringed Flower with Decorative Edge

Cut strip as for Basic Fringed Flower; trim one long edge with decorative-edge scissors. Make fringe cuts toward straight edge, then roll, adhere and fluff open as for a Basic Fringed Flower.

Spider Mum Fringed Flower

Form the flower using a wedge-shaped strip of paper, as it is the angle of the wedge that creates the varied length of the fringe. The strip may be any size, although a strip ¼ inch or wider gives the best result. An example would be a strip 3 inches long, ¼ inch wide at the narrow end and gradually increasing to ¾ inch wide at the other end. Snip the angled edge in a fine fringe, then roll the strip beginning at the wider end. Fluff open the layers of fringed petals.

Fringed Leaf

Cut a ½-inch square of paper; fold it in half on the diagonal. Cut a curved half-leaf shape starting at lowest point of fold. Open the leaf and shape tip in a natural curve.

Variation: With paper still folded, make tiny, angled snips along curved edge.

Folded Rose

A Folded Rose can be made with a strip of almost any width and length. A standard size strip would measure ⅜ x 7 inches. Narrower strips, such as ¼ inch or even ⅛ inch, would result in a smaller rose or bud.

Slip end of strip into slotted tool from the left. Holding the tool vertically in right hand and the strip in left hand, roll the tool clockwise to the left a few times to secure the paper. This will be the center of the rose.

With left hand, fold the paper strip up at a 90-degree angle. Continue to roll the tool toward the left, rolling over the fold. At the same time, gently lower the strip with left hand to return it to a horizontal position.

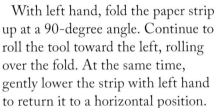

Repeat this folding-and-rolling process until you reach the end of the strip. Slip rose (which has formed upside down) off the tool, allow it to relax, and shape folds gently as desired. Snip off excess strip length and hide end by gluing it under rose.

Rectangle Rose

Rose center: Form a ½ x 1-inch strip into a Loose (Closed) Coil.

Petals: Cut 10 (¾ x 1-inch) rectangles. Make a slit halfway down the length of each rectangle. Overlap and adhere the two resulting "legs" to form a cup shape. Use tool to curl under the two corners on the uncut end of rectangle.

Assembly: Cut a dime-size circle of paper. Adhere four petals with curled ends facing outward from center to the perimeter of the circle. Let dry, then adhere four petals closer to the center, positioning each one between the petals of the first circle. Adhere remaining two petals still closer to the center, overlapping each other at the base. Insert and adhere the Loose (Closed) Coil as the rose center.

Spiral

Continuously wrap strip around a thin, stiff wire or needle tool without overlapping edges. While still on wire, hold each end of spiral and twist gently to tighten. Slide straight off tool.

On-Edge Stem

Adhere two strips together, one on top of the other, to make a double thickness for extra strength. When dry, curve strip slightly to resemble a natural stem.

Wheatear

Begin with a full-length strip. Fold down one end of strip ½ inch (measurement is an example only). Adhere end. Loop paper once around this fold; apply a tiny amount of glue at bottom of loop. Continue to wrap evenly spaced loops around bottom anchor point; each loop will be slightly taller than one preceding it. Form as many loops as desired.

Cut off excess paper and adhere end. Wheatear can be shaped by gently pinching and curving tip to create the look of foliage.

Alternate Side Loop (ASL)

Begin with a full-length strip. Fold down and adhere one end at the desired height of petal or leaf, creating a loop. Without cutting the strip, form another slightly shorter loop to the left of the center loop, and then one of matching height on the right side. Form a second pair of loops shorter than the first pair. Encircle all loops once, creating a collar. Adhere at bottom and cut off excess paper. Pinch and curve tip if desired.

Variations: 1. Form as many pairs of loops as desired. 2. Encircle all loops two or three times, leaving space between each collar. 3. Pinch tip and sides of collars.

Bright Butterflies

Design by **Sandy L. Rollinger**

Card

Cut a 4½ x 6½-inch piece of purple card stock; run through crimper so that grooves run vertically. Center and adhere crimped card stock to card front.

Cut two 7-inch pieces of light green quilling strip. Adhere one piece to card 1 inch from top; adhere second piece to card 1 inch from bottom.

Cut three 1½-inch squares from light green card stock. Center and adhere them to card front on the diagonal, evenly spaced, with ends of outer squares even with edges of card.

Quilled Butterflies

Wings: Cut four 3-inch pieces each of yellow, fuchsia and orange quilling strips. Form each into a Teardrop.

Bodies: Cut three 3-inch pieces from dark green quilling strips. Form each into a Marquise.

Antennae: Cut three 1-inch pieces of dark green quilling strips. Form each into a V Scroll.

Center and adhere a body and antennae to each light green square on card front. Adhere wings to squares as shown.

Source: Zip Dry Paper Glue from Beacon Adhesives Inc.

Materials
7 x 5-inch white top-fold greeting card
Card stock: light green, purple
⅛-inch-wide quilling paper strips: light green, dark green, yellow, fuchsia, orange
Slotted quilling tool
Tweezers
Paper crimper
Instant-dry paper glue

Project notes:
Refer to Shape Gallery, pages 5–7, throughout to form quilled shapes. Refer to photo throughout for placement.

Materials
Lime green card
   stock
⅛-inch-wide
   quilling paper
   strips: green,
   light green, red
4 inches ½-inch-
   wide white/red
   polka-dot paper
   ribbon
Slotted quilling tool
Tweezers
Paper crimper
Paper glue
Project notes:
*Refer to Shape
Gallery, pages 5–7,
throughout to form
quilled shapes. Refer
to photo throughout
for placement.*

Cheerful Cherries

Design by **Ann Martin**

Card

Cut a 5 x 3-inch piece of card stock. Score card stock vertically 2¼ inches from left edge; fold left flap over to form an asymmetrical side-fold card.

Crimp paper ribbon; adhere to right edge of card's back panel with edges even.

Quilled Cherries

Stems: Cut two 2½-inch pieces of green quilling strips; form into On-Edge Stem. When dry, cut stem into a 1-inch and a 1½-inch piece. Curve each piece slightly.

Leaves: Cut three 6-inch pieces of green quilling strips and two 4-inch pieces of light green quilling strips; form each into a Marquise.

Cherries: Cut one 10-inch piece and one 14-inch piece from red quilling strip; form each into a Loose (Closed) Coil.

Arrange cherries, stems and leaves on card front as shown; adhere to card.

Vines & Flourishes

Design by **Ann Martin**

Card

Form a 5½ x 4¼-inch top-fold card from card stock.

Cut a 5 x 3¾-inch piece of printed paper. Trim corners of printed paper on the diagonal using decorative-edge scissors; in the same manner, trim bottom corners on card front only. Ink trimmed edges on printed paper and card front using gel pen. Center and adhere printed paper to card front using double-sided tape.

Quilled Design

Scrolls: Using strips of quilling paper no longer than 3 inches, form a variety of Loose (Open) Scrolls, C Scrolls and S Scrolls.

Flowers: For each flower, form three Alternate Side Loop (ASL) petals of desired size and an Oval Tight Coil using a 3-inch piece of quilling strip. Assemble flower by adhering petals side by side, curving the tips of the two outer petals outward; adhere oval at base of flower.

Arrange and adhere flowers and scrolls on card front as desired. Mimic the pattern in the printed paper or create your own; there is no right or wrong way to form the design. It will look just as pretty with fewer quilled motifs as it does with many.

Materials

Hyacinth blue card stock
White-on-white scrolls printed paper
⅛-inch-wide hyacinth blue quilling paper strips
Silver gel pen
Slotted quilling tool
Tweezers
Decorative-edge scissors
Double-sided tape
Paper glue

Project notes:

Refer to Shape Gallery, pages 5–7, throughout to form quilled shapes. Refer to photo throughout for placement. Adhere elements using paper glue unless instructed otherwise.

Citrus Thanks

Design by **Susan Stringfellow**

Card

Form a 5½ x 4¼-inch top-fold card from printed paper.

Center Panel

Cut a 3½ x 2¼-inch rectangle from white card stock; tear across top edge.

Punch two holes in card stock ¾ inch from bottom and ¼ inch from each edge; attach eyelets in holes. Cut ribbon in half; tie one piece through each eyelet.

Stamp "thanks" in lower right corner of card stock.

Quilled Orange Slice

Segments: Cut four 8 x ¼-inch strips from orange card stock. Form each into a ⅝-inch Loose (Closed) Coil, then into a Triangle. Adhere segments edge to edge to form slice.

Center: Cut a 1 x ¼-inch strip from orange card stock. Form into a small Oval Tight Coil; flatten slightly and adhere to center of slice.

Orange peel: Cut a 4 x ¼-inch strip from white card stock. Run strip through crimper or accordion-fold strip every ⅛ inch. Adhere along curved edge of orange slice.

Cut two ¼-inch-wide strips from orange card stock; adhere to white crimped strip around curved edge; trim ends even.

Quilled Swirls

Cut four 4 x ¼-inch strips from light green card stock. Referring to Green Swirls pattern on page 46, form one piece into an S Scroll, one into a Loose (Open) Scroll, and one into a Heart Scroll; assemble according to pattern.

Finishing

Adhere orange slice to white card-stock panel; arrange and adhere light green scrolls to right of orange slice as shown. Center and adhere white card stock to card front.

Sources: Fresh Print printed paper from Déjà Views; Wordsworth stamp from Rubber Soul; eyelets from We R Memory Keepers.

Materials

Card stock: orange, white, light green

Mango floral printed paper

"Thanks" stamp

Black ink pad

2 light green ⅝-inch decorative eyelets

8 inches ⅜-inch-wide orange ribbon with white pin dots

Slotted quilling tool

Tweezers

Paper crimper (optional)

Eyelet-setting tool

¼-inch hole punch

Paper glue

Project notes:

Refer to Shape Gallery, pages 5–7, throughout to form quilled shapes. Refer to photo throughout for placement.

Peace & Hope

Design by **Allison Bartkowski,** *courtesy of Quilled Creations Inc.*

Materials

Card stock: navy blue, light blue, white

Light blue vellum

⅛-inch-wide quilling paper strips: white, leaf green

Leaves stamp

Blue ink pad

¼-inch black rub-on transfers: "Peace," "Hope"

Leaves punch

Slotted quilling tool

Tweezers

Adhesive tabs

Paper glue

Project notes:

Refer to Shape Gallery, pages 5–7, throughout to form quilled shapes. Refer to photo throughout for placement. Adhere elements using paper glue unless instructed otherwise.

Form a 4 x 5-inch top-fold card from light blue card stock; ink edges.

Cut a 3¾ x 4¾-inch rectangle from white card stock; stamp leaves on upper right and lower left corners. Center and adhere card stock to card.

Cut an 8 x 1¾-inch strip of vellum; wrap around card front 1½ inches from top; adhere ends inside card using adhesive tabs. Apply "Peace" and "Hope" rub-on transfers to vellum strip as shown; punch two leaves from navy blue card stock and adhere to vellum beside words.

Cut a 1¼-inch square from navy blue card stock; adhere to light blue card stock and trim, leaving ⅛-inch borders. Ink edges. Adhere squares to card front, overlapping vellum strip, ¼ inch from right edge and 1⅛ inches from bottom.

Quilled Dove

Body: Cut an 8-inch piece of white quilling strip and form into a Teardrop; pinch a second point to form tail.

Head: Cut a 4-inch piece of white quilling strip and form into a Teardrop.

Wing: Cut a 4-inch piece of white quilling strip in half lengthwise to form a ¹⁄₁₆-inch-wide strip; form into a Teardrop.

Olive branch: Cut a 4-inch piece of leaf green quilling strip in half lengthwise to form a ¹⁄₁₆-inch-wide strip. From this narrow strip, cut a 2-inch piece and form it into a Shaped Marquise for leaf; form the remaining piece into an S Scroll for stem.

Adhere dove's body and head to navy blue square on card front; adhere wing to body. Adhere stem and leaf to card stock at dove's beak.

Sources: Quilling paper strips from Quilled Creations Inc.; Leaves stamp from Paper Source; VersaMagic Dew Drop ink from Tsukineko Inc.; leaves punch from EK Success.

Hope it's
Berry Special!

Berry Happy Birthday

Design by **Loretta Mateik**

Materials

Card stock: red, embossed white dotted Swiss

⅛-inch-wide quilling paper strips: red, green

Plain white paper

"Happy Birthday" stamp approximately 3 x ⅝ inch

Red ink pad

Red fine-tip marker

4 inches ⅝-inch-wide sheer red ribbon

Slotted quilling tool

Tweezers

¼-inch hole punch

Removable tape

Paper glue

Computer and printer (optional)

Project notes:

Refer to Shape Gallery, pages 5–7, throughout to form quilled shapes. Refer to photo throughout for placement.

Card

Form a 4¾ x 3⅞-inch top-fold card from red card stock.

Lettering: Cut a 4⅜ x 3½-inch rectangle from dotted Swiss card stock; stamp "Happy Birthday" across bottom. ***Options:*** *Hand-print "Happy Birthday" using red marker; or use computer to generate sentiment onto plain white paper; adhere dotted Swiss card-stock rectangle over printing using removable tape so that lettering is centered along bottom and run through printer again, using red ink.*

Ribbon: Center and punch two holes in stamped card-stock rectangle ¼ inch apart and ¼ inch from top. Thread ribbon through holes; knot on front. Trim ends.

Quilled Strawberries

Copy or trace strawberry pattern on page 46 onto plain white paper to use as a template.

Berries: Cut 12-inch pieces of red quilling strips. Form each into a ⅜-inch Loose (Closed) Coil. Arrange circles inside template to form strawberry, making smaller Loose (Closed) Coils as needed to fill empty spaces and define shape. Adhere circles to one another. Repeat to make a second strawberry.

Leaves: Cut six 8-inch pieces of green quilling strips. Form each into a Marquise. Adhere three atop each strawberry as shown.

Stems: Cut two ⅝-inch pieces of green quilling strips. Curve each gently.

Adhere strawberries and stems to dotted Swiss card-stock rectangle as shown. Center and adhere card stock to card front.

Card Interior

Hand-print, or use computer to generate, birthday greeting on a 4¼ x 3⅜-inch rectangle cut from dotted Swiss card stock. Center and adhere inside card.

Sources: Embossed card stock from Lasting Impressions for Paper Inc.; quilling paper from Lake City Craft Company.

Baby Shower Invitation

Design by **Loretta Mateik**

Card

Form a 5½ x 4¼-inch top-fold card from white linen card stock.

Embossing

Lettering: Using letters from "It's a Boy" and "Baby Shower" on embossing templates, trace "to a Baby Shower" in reverse onto plain white paper to establish spacing. Trim paper with lettering so that it is 5½ inches wide and lettering is centered on the strip.

On the back of the card, lightly pencil a horizontal line ³⁄₁₆ inch from bottom. You will align the bottoms of all the embossed letters (except the *y*) along this line.

Using removable tape, tape the Baby Sayings embossing template to the light box or sunny window so that the lettering is backward. Lay your paper template on the template so that penciled *t* in "to" aligns with *t* on the embossing template; secure with removable tape.

Open the card and lay it right side down over template so that ends of paper strip are even with edges of card and the penciled line is even with the bottom of the *t*. Secure as needed with removable tape. Rub the card stock with waxed paper and emboss *t* with the stylus.

Move the paper template and the card to the next letter—*o*—and repeat. Repeat to emboss *a*.

When you emboss "Baby Shower," you can leave the templates in place to emboss the entire phrase.

Scalloped edge: Use scalloped edge of brass embossing template to emboss a scalloped edge on front flap of card ¾ inch from bottom, again embossing from the reverse side. Trim excess card stock from front flap below scalloped edge, leaving as narrow a margin as possible. Embossed lettering will now be visible when card is closed.

Rectangle: Embossing from the *right side* of the card and using straight edge of brass template, center and emboss a 4¾ x 3-inch rectangle on card's front flap.

Quilled Flower

Petals: Cut five 12-inch pieces of periwinkle blue quilling strips. Form each into a Teardrop.

Materials

Card stock: white linen, light green, embossed white dotted Swiss

⅛-inch-wide quilling paper strips: periwinkle blue, off-white

Plain white paper

Blue chalk

Blue fine-tip marker

14 inches ⅜-inch-wide sheer blue ribbon

Embossing templates: Buttons and Bow, Baby Sayings

Waxed paper

Embossing stylus

Slotted quilling tool

Tweezers

Decorative-edge scissors

Light box or sunny window

Removable tape

¹⁄₁₆-inch adhesive foam dots

Paper glue

Computer and printer (optional)

Project notes:

Refer to Shape Gallery, pages 5–7, throughout to form quilled shapes. Refer to photo throughout for placement. Adhere elements using paper glue unless instructed otherwise.

Flower center: Cut an 8-inch piece of off-white quilling strip. Form into a ⅜-inch Loose (Closed) Coil.

Leaves: Referring to pattern on page 46, cut three leaves from light green card stock. Lightly emboss center vein on each and snip edges, curling them slightly.

Assembly

Wrap ribbon around card's front flap 1½ inches from fold. Knot ends on front 2 inches from right edge; trim ends as desired.

Hand-print, or use computer to generate, "You're invited!" in blue ink on dotted Swiss card stock to fit within an area 1 x ⅝ inch. Trim a 2 x 1⅜-inch rectangle around words using decorative-edge scissors; chalk edges. Adhere rectangle to card at an angle using adhesive foam dots.

Arrange leaves on card front, overlapping ribbon; adhere. Arrange and adhere flower petals to card around flower center.

Card Interior

Hand-print, or use a computer to generate, baby shower details in blue ink on dotted Swiss card stock to fit inside card. Trim rectangle around lettering; chalk edges. Adhere inside card.

Sources: Embossed card stock and embossing templates from Lasting Impressions for Paper Inc.; quilling paper from Lake City Craft Company.

Butterfly Tag

Design by **Allison Bartkowski,** *courtesy of Quilled Creations Inc.*

Quilled Butterflies

Pink wings: Position five pins in the work board according to Fig. 1. Bend a tiny loop in one end of a 6-inch piece of pink quilling strip; secure with a drop of glue. Anchor loop around pin no. 1. Loop the pink paper strip around pin no. 2, then back around pin no. 1. Secure the paper strip with a drop of glue below pin no. 1, or wherever paper strip touches and overlaps (Fig. 2).

Continue looping and gluing the paper strip around pins no. 3, 4 and 5 in order (Fig. 3). Make one final wrap around all the pins, and secure the paper strip below pin no. 1 using a drop of glue (Fig. 4). Trim off any extra paper. Pinch the tip of the wing, if desired. Repeat to make a second pink wing.

Purple wings: Follow instructions for pink wings using two pieces of purple quilling strips. Pinch the tips of the wings if desired, or leave them unpinched for a more rounded appearance.

Butterfly bodies: Cut two 4-inch pieces of light green quilling strips and form each into a Teardrop.

Butterfly heads: Cut two 2-inch pieces of light green quilling strips and form each into a into a Loose (Closed) Coil.

Antennae: Cut two ½-inch pieces of light green quilling strips; fold each in half.

Assembly & Finishing

Butterflies: Assemble butterflies and attach them to the tag as shown. Draw their dashed-line "flight paths" using fine-tip marker.

Using marker, write message on a small strip of printed paper; punch hole in each end of strip and attach to tag using mini flower brads.

Cut ⅛-inch-wide strips from the printed paper; loop the strips through the hole in the tag. Curl ends of strips over a scissors blade. ∎

Source: Quilling paper strips from Quilled Creations Inc.

Materials

- 2½ x 5-inch lavender card-stock tag
- Green-and-white gingham check printed paper
- ⅛-inch-wide quilling paper strips: light green, purple, pink
- Fine-tip black marker or pen
- 2 mini flower brads
- Slotted quilling tool
- Tweezers
- Work board
- Straight pins
- 1⁄16-inch hole punch
- Instant-dry paper glue

Project notes:
Refer to Shape Gallery, pages 5–7, throughout to form quilled shapes. Refer to photo throughout for placement.

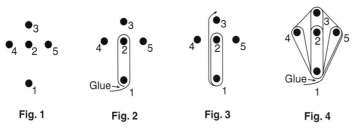

Fig. 1   **Fig. 2**   **Fig. 3**   **Fig. 4**

Rose Bouquet

Design by **Ann Martin**

Card

Outline opening using gel pen if desired. Cut gold metallic paper to fit card panel with opening; adhere to reverse side using double-sided tape.

Quilled Bouquet

Bouquet wrapper: Cut a 3-inch-tall wedge from vellum that measures 4 inches across top and 1 inch across bottom. Lay right side down. Without creasing vellum, gently fold in thirds, bending sides toward center with left side overlapping right to create wrapper; trim left edge with decorative-edge scissors.

Roses: Form quilling paper into a variety of Folded Roses using both widths and all colors. Arrange roses randomly to form bouquet, adhering them to metallic gold paper and vellum wrapper.

Leaves: Cut 10 (½-inch) squares from leaf green card stock. Fold each in half diagonally. Holding each piece on the fold, cut edges in a curved leaf shape; open leaf, then pinch top point for a realistic look.

Tendrils: Cut several 3-inch pieces from ⅛-inch-wide quilling strips in a variety of colors; form each into a Loose (Open) Scroll.

Use tweezers to tuck leaves and tendrils into arrangement as desired; adhere.

Materials

4 x 6-inch white card with 2½ x 4-inch oval opening
Leaf green lightweight card stock
Gold metallic paper
White-on-white printed vellum
Quilling paper strips:
⅛-inch-wide dark peach, peach, pale peach
¼-inch-wide dark peach, peach, pale peach
Gold metallic gel pen (optional)
Slotted quilling tool
Tweezers
Decorative-edge scissors
Double-sided tape
Paper glue

Project notes:

Refer to Shape Gallery, pages 5–7, throughout to form quilled shapes. Refer to photo throughout for placement. Adhere elements using paper glue unless instructed otherwise.

Snowflake Ornament

Design by **Allison Bartkowski,** *courtesy of Quilled Creations Inc.*

Card

Form a 4 x 5-inch side-fold card from navy blue card stock.

Cut a 3 x 4¾-inch piece of printed paper; adhere to medium blue card stock and trim, leaving even ⅛-inch borders. Wrap medium blue satin ribbon around panel ⅝ inch from top; knot ribbon ends on front near left; trim ribbon ends at an angle.

Quilled Snowflake Ornament

Snowflake arms: Cut six 8-inch pieces of quilling strips and form each into a Marquise.

Snowflake ends: Cut six 4-inch pieces of quilling strips and form each into a Heart Scroll.

Arrange and adhere snowflake arms to each other; adhere ends to arms as shown. Brush top of snowflake with paint.

Thread navy blue ribbon through one end of snowflake; affix ribbon ends to paper/card-stock panel as shown using a ³⁄₁₆-inch rhinestone brad. Center and adhere panel with ornament to card ⅝ inch from right edge.

Attach ⁵⁄₁₆-inch and ¼-inch rhinestone brads to card's lower right corner as shown. Paint card edges with paint.

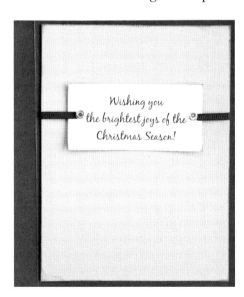

Card Interior

Cut a 3¾ x 5-inch rectangle from medium blue card stock; ink edges.

Hand-print, or use computer to generate, Christmas sentiment on white card stock to fit within an area measuring 2 x 1 inch; trim 2¾ x 1¼-inch tag around words; ink edges.

Center and punch a hole in each end of tag ¼ inch from edge; thread navy blue ribbon through holes and add ³⁄₁₆-inch brads.

Center and adhere tag to medium blue card stock 1¼ inches from top; wrap ribbon ends around to back and secure on reverse side with adhesive tabs. Center and adhere card stock with tag to card.

Envelope

Cut a 2 x 4¼-inch rectangle from printed paper; rub paint over edges. Embellish with snowflakes punched from white card stock.

Source: Beginner Quilling Kit snowflake design and WaterSparklers paints from Quilled Creations Inc.

Materials

Card stock: navy blue, medium blue, white

Blue-on-blue family sentiments printed paper

White ⅛-inch-wide quilling paper strips

5¾ x 4½-inch white envelope

Light blue iridescent craft paint

Blue ink pad

Fine-tip black marker

Ribbon:
8 inches ½-inch-wide medium blue silk
5 inches ⅛-inch-wide navy blue grosgrain

Rhinestone brads: ⁵⁄₁₆-inch, ¼-inch, 3 (³⁄₁₆-inch)

Small paintbrush

Slotted quilling tool

Tweezers

Punches: ¹⁄₁₆-inch or ⅛-inch hole, assorted ⅜-inch snowflakes

Adhesive tabs

Paper glue

Computer and printer (optional)

Project notes:

Refer to Shape Gallery, pages 5–7, throughout to form quilled shapes. Refer to photo throughout for placement. Adhere elements with paper glue unless instructed otherwise.

Sand Dollar

Design by **Ann Martin**

Pocket

Cut a 4¼ x 9-inch piece of card stock. Score card stock horizontally 3¾ inches from bottom; fold up. Adhere side edges only to form pocket.

Cut a 4¼ x 1¾-inch piece of embossed paper; adhere to top edge of pocket front. Cut a 4¼ x 1-inch strip from striped printed paper with stripes running vertically; center and adhere to embossed paper strip. Adhere 4¼-inch pieces of brown quilling strips over top and bottom edges of striped strip. Center and adhere charms to striped strip.

Tag

Cut a 3½ x 5-inch tag from card stock. Set eyelet, centered, near edge of narrow end; loop ribbon through eyelet and trim ribbon ends. Tuck tag into pocket.

Quilled Sand Dollar

Base: Crimp several pieces of brown and yellow quilling strips, running them through the crimper several strips at a time so that they are not cut into confetti.

Insert a yellow crimped strip and a brown crimped strip into the quilling tool at the same time; roll gently to avoid compressing crimps. When you reach the end, adhere two more strips and continue. Continue rolling and adding strips until base measures 2 inches in diameter. Adhere ends.

Wrap base with brown crimped strip; adhere. Apply a thin coat of glue to back of entire base for stability.

Star arms: Cut five 8-inch pieces of brown quilling strips; form each into a Teardrop.

Star center: Cut a 3½-inch piece of brown quilling strip; form into a Grape Roll.

Ovals: Using brown quilling paper, form four small Ring Coils, wrapping paper a few times around crochet hook. Pinch completed Ring Coils to form ovals.

Make one larger Ring Coil from brown quilling paper by wrapping it a few times around the larger handle of the quilling tool; pinch into an oval.

Assembly

Using tweezers, press front surface of the sand dollar base, star arms, star center and ovals onto ink pad.

Adhere base to pocket in lower right corner as shown; arrange and adhere star arms and center to base. Adhere large oval to base between bottom two arms; adhere remaining ovals to base at ends of all arms except top arm.

Materials

Pale yellow card stock

Printed paper: cream embossed with dots, yellow/brown/white stripe

⅛-inch-wide quilling paper strips: yellow, brown

Gold metallic ink pad

8 inches 5⁄16-inch-wide pale yellow grosgrain ribbon

Silver eyelet

3 (5⁄8-inch) seashore charms

Slotted quilling tool

Tweezers

Paper crimper

Glass-head pin

Eyelet-setting tool

Crochet hook or similar object that is smaller in diameter than quilling tool

Paper glue

Project notes:
Refer to Shape Gallery, pages 5–7, throughout to form quilled shapes. Refer to photo throughout for placement.

Autumn Bouquet

Design by **Ann Martin**

Materials

- Speckled off-white card stock
- Brown kraft paper
- Quilling paper strips:
  - ⅛-inch-wide red, yellow, gold
  - ¼-inch-wide yellow, gold
  - ⅜-inch-wide yellow, gold, orange
  - ½-inch-wide orange
- Slotted quilling tool
- Orangewood stick or pen
- Tweezers
- Decorative-edge scissors
- Thin, stiff wire or needle tool
- Work board
- Straight pins
- Paper crimper
- Paper glue

Project notes:
Refer to Shape Gallery, pages 5–7, throughout to form quilled shapes. Refer to photo throughout for placement.

Card

Form a 5 x 7-inch side-fold card from card stock.

Cut 4¼ x 6-inch piece of kraft paper; crimp horizontally. Center and adhere to card front.

Cut 2¾ x 4½-inch piece of card stock; trim top and bottom edges with decorative-edge scissors. Center and adhere card stock to crimped kraft paper.

Quilled Bouquet

Roses: Form two Folded Roses from yellow ⅜-inch-wide quilling strips. Form one Folded Rose each from gold ⅜-inch-wide, yellow ¼-inch-wide and gold ¼-inch-wide quilling strips.

Mums: Cut a 3-inch piece of orange ½-inch-wide quilling strip and a 3-inch piece of yellow ⅛-inch-wide quilling strip; glue pieces together and form into a Basic Fringed Flower with yellow section in center.

Cut a 3-inch piece of orange ⅜-inch-wide quilling strip and a 3-inch piece of yellow ⅛-inch-wide quilling strip; glue pieces together and form into a Fringed Flower with Tight Coil Center, shaping center into a dome.

Cut a 3-inch piece of gold ⅜-inch-wide quilling strip and a 3-inch piece of red ⅛-inch-wide quilling strip; glue pieces together and form into a Fringed Flower with Tight Coil Center, shaping center into a dome.

Teardrop flowers with buds: Cut six 4-inch pieces from red ⅛-inch-wide quilling strips; form each into a Teardrop. Form one Alternate Side Loop (ASL) petal from a piece of yellow ⅛-inch-wide quilling strip and another from a piece of gold ⅛-inch-wide quilling strip.

Cut two 4-inch pieces from gold ⅛-inch-wide quilling strips; form each into a Grape Roll.

Form one teardrop flower from two red Teardrops and the yellow ASL petal; form a second from the remaining red teardrops and the gold ASL petal.

Adhere rounded end of one of the remaining red Teardrop petals to each Grape Roll.

Tendrils: Cut six 1½-inch pieces of ⅛-inch-wide quilling strips in assorted colors; form three into Loose (Open) Scrolls and three into Spirals.

Six-petal flowers: Cut six 2½-inch pieces from red ⅛-inch-wide quilling strips; form each into a Teardrop. Cut a 2-inch piece from yellow ⅛-inch-wide quilling strip; form into a Sculptured Tight Coil. Arrange petals with broad ends touching; adhere to one another. Adhere Sculptured Tight Coil in center of flower.

Cut six 2½-inch pieces from gold ⅛-inch-wide quilling strips; form each into a Teardrop. Cut a 2-inch piece from red ⅛-inch-wide quilling strip; form into a Tight Coil. Arrange petals with broad ends touching; adhere to one another. Adhere Tight Coil in center of flower.

Assembly

Arrange roses and mums on card front as desired; adhere. Using tweezers, add remaining flowers and tuck tendrils into arrangement as desired; adhere.

Party Favor Purses

Design by **Molly M. Smith**

Quilled flower: Cut five 3-inch pieces from matching quilling strips. Referring to Shape Gallery, pages 5–7, form each into a quilled Teardrop measuring a scant ⅜ inch. Arrange and adhere Teardrops with points touching in center to form flower. Center and adhere rhinestone to center of flower.

Purse: Cut a 5 x 1½-inch piece of printed paper; lay facedown. Referring to diagram on page 46, score paper vertically 1½ inches, 2½ inches and 4 inches from left edge. Round off corners on right edge. Punch holes over 4-inch scored line ¼ inch from top and bottom edges. Ink edges if desired.

Materials

Printed paper: colors and/or metallics

⅛-inch-wide quilling paper strips: complementary solid colors and/or white with metallic gold edges

Complementary ink pad or marker (optional)

Complementary ⅛- to ¼-inch-wide ribbons

2.5mm flat-back crystal rhinestones

Silver- and gold-wrapped chocolate nuggets

Slotted quilling tool

Tweezers

Punches: ¹⁄₁₆-inch hole, corner rounder

Tape: adhesive, double-sided

Paper glue

Project notes:

Refer to Shape Gallery, pages 5–7, throughout to form quilled shapes. Refer to photo throughout for placement. Adhere elements using paper glue unless instructed otherwise.

Thread ends of a 3-inch piece of ribbon through holes; tape ¼ inch of ends to wrong (plain) side. Fold purse closed; adhere flap to purse front using double-sided tape.

Adhere quilled flower to purse flap as shown. Affix double-sided tape to bottom of chocolate nugget; slide inside purse and press onto bottom to secure.

Sources: Paper Passport Collage Pad metallic printed paper from Provo Craft; quilling paper strips from Whimsiquills.

Birthday Gift Set

Designs by **Allison Bartkowski,** *courtesy of Quilled Creations Inc.*

Card

Form a 4 x 5-inch side-folded card from textured white card stock. Cut a 3⁹⁄₁₆ x 4½-inch piece from printed paper and a 3⅞ x 4¾-inch rectangle from textured light blue card stock; center and adhere printed paper to card stock; center and adhere joined pieces to card.

Birthday cake: Cut a 2 x 1½-inch piece from textured white card stock; trim top edge with decorative-edge scissors; round off bottom corners. Wrap yellow and turquoise rickrack across cake as shown, wrapping ends over edge and adhering to reverse side. Center and adhere cake to card using glue dots.

Candles: Cut one 8-inch piece each from deep blue, light blue and lime green quilling strips. Form each into a Rectangle for candle. Cut three 4-inch pieces from deep yellow quilling strips; form each into a Shaped Teardrop for flame. Adhere candles and flames to card at top of cake.

"Make a Wish!": Cut a 3¼ x ⁹⁄₁₆-inch strip from plain white card stock. Apply rub-on transfers to spell "Make a Wish!," leaving room at ends and between words for mini brads. Center and adhere strip to card ⅜ inch from bottom edge.

Punch ¹⁄₁₆-inch holes at ends of strip and between words; affix yellow mini brads in ends and rose and teal mini brads between words.

Gift Bag

Referring to diagram on page 47, form a flat-bottom gift bag from a 12 x 8-inch piece of textured white card stock, scoring and folding card stock along dashed lines. Adhere adjacent surfaces as needed so that bag will hold its shape.

Cut a 4 x 1½-inch strip from printed paper; adhere to gift bag 1½ inches from top. Adhere orange rickrack across bottom edge of paper strip, wrapping ends over edges and adhering to reverse side.

Tag: Apply rub-on transfers to spell "Celebrate" onto plain white card stock; punch a 1⅜-inch circle around word. Adhere circle to brown card stock; trim, leaving

narrow border. Punch a ¹⁄₁₆-inch hole in center top of tag; affix deep yellow mini brad in hole, piercing a folded length of lime green rickrack. Adhere tag to right side of paper strip as shown.

Candles: Make three quilled candles as for card; adhere to printed paper strip to left of "Celebrate!" tag.

Close bag using decorative paper clip.

Gift Tag

Cut a 2½ x 4-inch piece from printed paper; trim ½ inch off upper corners to create tag shape. Adhere tag to brown card stock; trim, leaving even narrow borders. Center and punch a ¼-inch hole ⅝ inch from top edge; double a 6-inch piece of turquoise rickrack and knot through hole.

Cut a 2 x 3-inch piece of textured white card stock. Wrap orange and lime green rickrack around card stock ⅜ inch and ⅞ inch from bottom as shown, wrapping ends over edge and adhering to reverse side. Center and adhere card stock to tag ⅜ inch from bottom using glue dots.

Candle: Form one deep blue quilled candle with flame as for card; adhere to tag ¾ inch from right edge as shown.

Sources: Printed paper from SEI; quilling paper strips from Quilled Creations Inc.

Materials

Card stock: brown, plain white, textured white, textured light blue

Light green/ multicolored dots printed paper

⅛-inch-wide quilling paper strips: deep blue, light blue, lime green, deep yellow

³⁄₁₆- to ¼-inch black alphabet rub-on transfers

Mini brads: rose, teal, 3 deep yellow

Rickrack: orange, yellow, lime green, turquoise

Green decorative paper clip

Slotted quilling tool

Tweezers

Punches: ¹⁄₁₆-inch hole, ¼-inch hole, 1⅜-inch circle

Decorative-edge scissors

Glue: paper glue, glue dots

Project notes:

Refer to Shape Gallery, pages 5–7, throughout to form quilled shapes. Refer to photo throughout for placement. Adhere elements using paper glue unless instructed otherwise.

Gone Fishing

Designs by **Sandy L. Rollinger**

Gift Bag

Cut a 6½ x 4-inch rectangle from gold card stock and another piece the same size from brass card stock; center pieces and adhere them, edge to edge, to gift bag.

Cut a 6¼ x ¾-inch strip from silver card stock; center and adhere to bag over seam between gold and brass card stock.

Cut three 2½ x 2¼-inch rectangles from silver card stock; adhere them to bag in a vertical row as shown, spacing them evenly.

Quilled Fish

Bodies: Cut three 8-inch pieces of gold quilling strips; form each into a Teardrop and indent broad end for mouth.

Tail fins: Cut three 4-inch pieces of gold quilling strips; form each into a Marquise and press points between finger and thumb to flatten them.

Dorsal fins: Cut three 2½-inch pieces of gold quilling strips; form each into a Teardrop and flatten broad end.

Bottom fins: Cut three 2½-inch pieces of gold quilling strips; form each into a Teardrop.

Quilled Corners

Cut four 8-inch pieces of silver quilling strips; form each into a V Scroll.

Finishing

Fish: On each silver rectangle on bag, arrange and adhere a fish body, tail fin, dorsal fin and bottom fin as shown, alternating directions of fish. Adhere three gold flat-back beads, rising like "bubbles" from fishes' mouths.

Corners: In each corner of background panel, arrange and adhere a silver V Scroll as shown; adhere a silver flat-back bead at the point of each V Scroll. Center and adhere remaining silver flat-back beads to ends of silver card-stock strip.

Gift Tag

Card: Form a 3 x 3¼-inch top-folded card from gold card stock. Cut a 2¼ x 2½-inch rectangle from silver card stock; center and adhere to gift tag.

Materials
Metallic card stock: silver, gold, brass
⅛-inch-wide metallic quilling paper strips: silver, gold
8 x 10-inch brown corrugated gift bag
10 inches ¼-inch-wide silver metallic ribbon
Small flat-back beads: 10 silver, 12 gold
Slotted quilling tool
Tweezers
Instant-dry paper glue

Project notes:
Refer to Shape Gallery, pages 5–7, throughout to form quilled shapes. Refer to photo throughout for placement.

Fish: Cut two 4½-inch pieces of gold card stock. Form one into a Teardrop for fish's body and other piece into a Marquise for tail.

Adhere body and tail to tag as shown. Adhere three gold flat-back beads, rising like "bubbles" from fish's mouth. Adhere a silver flat-back bead in each corner of silver card-stock rectangle.

Center tag on ribbon; adhere ribbon inside card along fold. Tie card to gift bag handle or package.

Sources: Metallic Stack card stock from Die Cuts With A View; beads from The Robins Nest; Zip Dry Paper Glue from Beacon Adhesives Inc.

Fresh Floral Gift Set

Designs by **Sandy L. Rollinger**

Gift Bag

Center panel: Cut a 5½ x 7-inch piece from white card stock; center and punch border design in all four sides ³⁄₁₆ inch from edge.

Cut two 5½-inch pieces and two 7-inch pieces from blue quilling strips; adhere to white card stock ¾ inch from edges. Center and adhere card stock to bag.

Cut a 2½ x 3½-inch rectangle from blue card stock; center and adhere to white card-stock panel.

Punched flowers: Punch eight flowers from white card stock and four flowers from blue card stock. Center and adhere four white flowers over intersections of blue quilling strips. Center and adhere remaining white flowers to blue flowers, alternating positions of petals; adhere over corners of center blue rectangle.

Quilled Flower

Petals: Cut three 8-inch pieces of white quilling strips; form each into a Teardrop.

Greenery: Using green quilling strips throughout, cut one 2½-inch piece; form into a Teardrop. Indent rounded base (Shaped Teardrop) to form calyx for flower. Cut one 2-inch piece; form into a Teardrop for leaf. Cut one 1½-inch piece; form into a smaller Teardrop for smaller leaf. Cut one 2-inch piece; form into S Scroll for stem.

Finishing

Arrange and adhere flower with calyx, leaves and stem on blue rectangle as shown. Adhere flat-back beads to center of each punched flower; arrange and adhere five more beads over top of quilled flower.

Gift Tag

Card: Form a 2½ x 3¼-inch top-folded card from white card stock; trim ¼ inch off bottom edge of card front only. Center and punch border on front flap ³⁄₁₆ inch from bottom.

Cut two 2 x 1-inch rectangles from blue card stock; glue one inside card with bottom and side edges even. Turn other rectangle on end; center and adhere to front of tag.

Flower: Punch one flower from white card stock. Cut one 2-inch piece of green quilling strip; form into a Loose (Open) Scroll for stem. Cut one 1½-inch piece from green quilling strip; form into Teardrop for leaf.

Adhere stem and leaf to blue card stock on tag as shown; adhere punched flower. Adhere flat-backed bead to flower.

Center and punch a hole through top of tag near edge; thread craft cord through hole and tie to gift bag handle or package.

Sources: Beads from The Robins Nest; Paper Shapers flower punch from EK Success; Elegance border punch from Fiskars; Zip Dry Paper Glue from Beacon Adhesives Inc.

Materials

Card stock: blue, white

⅛-inch-wide quilling paper strips: white, blue, green

8 x 10-inch blue paper gift bag

12 inches white iridescent craft cord

9 pearl flat-back beads

Punches: Flower Power, Elegance border

Slotted quilling tool

Tweezers

¼-inch hole punch

Instant-dry paper glue

Project notes:

Refer to Shape Gallery, pages 5–7, throughout to form quilled shapes. Refer to photo throughout for placement.

Materials

Fuchsia card stock
⅛-inch-wide
   quilling paper
   strips: fuchsia,
   yellow, green
7 x 9¼-inch
   yellow-gold
   paper gift bag
Slotted quilling tool
Tweezers
¼-inch hole punch
Paper glue

Project notes:
Refer to Shape
Gallery, pages 5–7,
throughout to form
quilled shapes. Refer
to photo throughout
for placement.

Floral Gift Bag

Design by **Sherry Crocker**

Quilled Flowers

Flower petals: Cut 12 (12-inch) pieces of fuchsia quilling strips; form each into a Teardrop.

Flower centers: Cut two 24-inch pieces of yellow quilling strips; form each into a Tight Coil.

Leaves: Cut five 12-inch pieces of green quilling strips; form each into a Teardrop.

Stems: Cut two 1½–2¼-inch pieces of green quilling strips 1½–2¼ inches long.

Gift Bag Assembly

Adhere flower petals to gift bag in two groups of six with points touching, tucking ends of stems under petals. Adhere flower centers over petals.

Adhere leaves along stems as desired.

Fold 1-inch strips of green quilling paper into *V*'s; adhere to bag for grass.

Gift Tag

Referring to flower pattern on page 47, trace and cut flower from fuchsia card stock. Cut a 24-inch piece of yellow quilling strip and form into a ⅞-inch Loose (Closed) Coil; adhere to center of flower. Punch hole near edge of flower; tie tag to bag handle using a green quilling strip.

Calla Lily Gift Box

Design by **Allison Bartkowski,** *courtesy of Quilled Creations Inc.*

Lilies: Cut two 1-inch-tall teardrops from white card stock; position them on work surface with points at top. Lightly chalk centers and rounded edges. Curl rounded edges toward each other, forming a point at base of lily.

Stems: Apply glue to one end of a 3-inch piece of moss green quilling strip. Position it on edge with the glued end in the bottom of a white teardrop lily; press the curled sides into the glue and hold until the glue sets. In the same manner, using a 1-inch piece of moss green quilling strip, add a stem to the remaining lily.

Form the end of the longer stem into a Loose (Open) Scroll.

Flower centers: Cut two 2-inch pieces of white quilling strips; roll each into a Sculptured Tight Coil, and secure the ends with a drop of glue. Adhere a flower center inside each lily as shown.

Adhere lilies and stems to box lid.

Lily leaves: Form two pieces of moss green quilling strips into 4-loop Wheatears; adhere to box lid as shown.

Border leaves: Form six 5-loop Wheatears and two 3-loop Wheatears from moss green quilling strips. Roll four 2-inch pieces of white quilling strips into Tight Coils.

Adhere leaves to lid in pairs as shown, centering 3-loop leaves at top; adhere a white Tight Coil to lid between the leaves in each pair.

Source: Quilling paper strips from Quilled Creations Inc.

Materials

White card stock
⅛-inch-wide quilling paper strips: moss green, white
3-inch heart-shaped papier-mâché box with lid
Moss green chalk
Slotted quilling tool
Tweezers
Pen or orangewood stick
Paper glue

Project notes:
Refer to Shape Gallery, pages 5–7, throughout to form quilled shapes. Refer to photo throughout for placement.

Floral Note Pad

Design by **Susan Stringfellow**

Open matchbook note pad; lay flat on wrong side of multicolored blocks paper. Trace around note pad; cut out shape and adhere to note pad cover.

Close note pad. Tie rickrack around small flap near fold; secure with dots of glue as needed and trim ends.

Cut a 2-inch square from green pin-dot paper; adhere to orange paper and cut out, leaving ⅛-inch borders. Center and adhere to note pad.

Cut a 1¼-inch orange flower and a 2⅛-inch blue/green flower from floral printed paper; curve edges of petals slightly over the blade of scissors. Center and adhere center of larger flower to green pin-dot square; adhere center of smaller flower to upper left corner of central motif as shown.

Quilled flowers: Cut a 4 x ¾-inch strip of yellow card stock and form a Fringed Flower with Decorative Edge, inking the decorative edge before making fringe cuts.

Cut a 3 x ½-inch strip from yellow card stock; form a second Fringed Flower with Decorative Edge.

Gently bend center petals outward and adhere a rhinestone in the center of each flower using glitter glue. Center and adhere quilled flowers to the flowers cut from printed paper.

Quilled tendrils: Cut three 5 x ⅛-inch strips from light green card stock; form each into a Loose (Open) Scroll. Arrange on note pad as shown, trimming as desired and adhering ends under petals of larger flower.

Sources: Fresh Print printed papers from Déjà Views; decorative-edge scissors from Fiskars; Stickles glitter glue from Ranger Industries.

Materials

Card stock: yellow and light green to match colors on printed paper

Mango collection printed papers: multicolored blocks, orange solid, white/green mini pin dots, floral

3 x 4-inch matchbook-style note pad

Orange ink

2 (⅛-inch) orange rhinestones

9 inches orange rickrack

Mini scalloped decorative-edge scissors #92137097

Slotted quilling tool

Tweezers

Orange glitter glue

Paper glue

Project notes:

Refer to Shape Gallery, pages 5–7, throughout to form quilled shapes. Refer to photo throughout for placement. Adhere elements using paper glue unless instructed otherwise.

Framed Dragonflies

Designs by **Lori Mondell**

Quilled Dragonflies

Heads: Cut two 6-inch pieces from purple quilling strips. Form each into a Loose (Closed) Coil.

Crescents: Cut two 4-inch pieces from purple quilling strips. Form each into a Crescent.

Body: Cut four 7-inch pieces, four 5-inch pieces and four 3-inch pieces from purple quilling strips. Form each into a Tight Coil.

Upper wings: Cut eight 7-inch pieces from turquoise quilling strips. Form each into a Shaped Marquise.

Lower wings: Cut four 7-inch pieces from lime green quilling strips. Form each into a Teardrop.

Assembly

Cut two 2½ x 3½-inch rectangles from white linen paper; ink edges lightly. Stamp "Delight in Life" near top of one piece and "Happiness" sentiment toward bottom of the other.

Arrange and assemble dragonflies as shown, using one head, one crescent, two of each of the body coils, four upper wing sections and two lower wing sections for each.

Fold a floral stamen in half; trim to size and adhere to back of dragonfly's head.

Brush a very light coat of glue on the reverse side of the entire assembled dragonfly; adhere to stamped white linen paper.

Adhere gems to sections of dragonfly bodies and white linen paper as shown.

Adhere finished layouts to top of glass from frames using double-sided tape. Place glass in frames.

Sources: Paper from Provo Craft; stamps from Stampin' Up!

Materials

White linen textured paper
⅛-inch-wide quilling paper strips: purple, lime green, turquoise
2 (2½ x 3½-inch) black metal frames
Sentiment stamps: "Delight in Life," "Happiness"
Black ink
50–60 (2mm) crystal gems
4 black floral stamens
Slotted quilling tool
Tweezers
Small paintbrush
Double-sided tape
Paper glue

Project notes:
Refer to Shape Gallery, pages 5–7, throughout to form quilled shapes. Refer to photo throughout for placement. Adhere elements using paper glue unless instructed otherwise.

Materials

Teal Stripes printed
  paper
Quilling paper
  strips:
  ⅛-inch-wide
  light brown,
  red, turquoise,
  dark green, blue,
  yellow
  ⅜-inch-wide
  yellow
Thin cardboard
Wooden frame
  with opening for
  5 x 7-inch picture
Red paint
Sandpaper
Paintbrush
Slotted quilling tool
Tweezers
Paper glue
CD with Victorian-
  style font
Computer and
  printer

Project notes:
*Refer to Shape
Gallery, pages 5–7,
throughout to form
quilled shapes. Refer
to photo throughout
for placement.*

Monogram
Picture

Design by **Barbara Greve**

Sand and paint the frame.

Use computer and font CD to generate desired monogram on printed paper. ***Note:*** *On sample project, monogram measures approximately 3⅛ x 3 inches, not including the decorative flourishes and scrollwork.* Trim paper to fit in frame opening, centering monogram. Trim thin cardboard to same size; adhere printed paper to cardboard. Mount in frame.

Quilled Shapes

Scrollwork: Form eight to 10 light brown quilling strips into assorted Loose (Open) Scrolls, C Scrolls, and S Scrolls, mimicking the shapes of underlying printed scrollwork as desired; arrange and adhere scrolls to printed paper background.

Coiled flowers: Form 3-inch pieces of ⅛-inch-wide dark green, turquoise, blue, red and yellow quilling strips into Marquises and Bunny Ears Coils for leaves and flower petals, and Tight Coils for flower centers. Adhere flowers and leaves to background, attaching some flowers on top of others in layers.

Fringed flowers: Form 5- and 3-inch pieces of ⅜-inch-wide yellow quilling strips into Basic Fringed Flowers. Adhere them to layout as desired.

Sources: Kim Hodges printed paper from K&Company; Victorian Decorative Letters CD from Dover Publications.

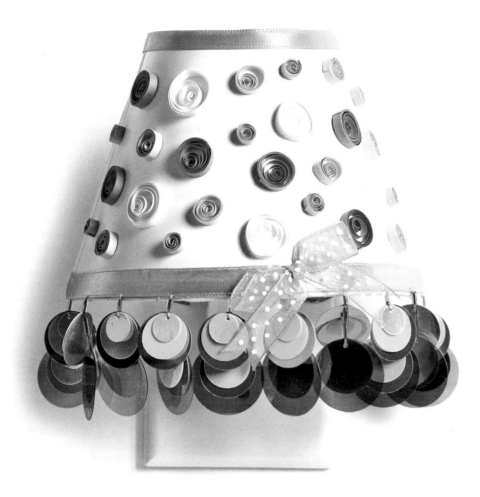

Night Light

Design by **Mary Ayres**

Materials
⅛-inch-wide
  quilling paper
  strips: white,
  mint green, light
  turquoise, dark
  turquoise
Night light with
  lamp shade
Ribbon:
  10 inches
  ⅜-inch-wide
  turquoise ribbon
  with green and
  blue spangles
  8 inches
  ¼-inch-wide
  turquoise
  10 inches
  ½-inch-wide
  sheer green with
  white pin dots
Slotted quilling tool
Tweezers
Circle template
Permanent adhesive
Project note:
*Refer to Shape
Gallery, pages 5–7,
throughout to form
quilled shapes.*

Adhere ribbon with spangles along bottom edge of shade and plain turquoise ribbon along top edge of shade, wrapping ribbon ends over edges and adhering them to reverse side.

Quilled circles: Cut five 12-inch pieces from white quilling strips. Form each into a ⅝-inch Loose (Closed) Coil.

In the same manner, form eight 6-inch pieces of mint green quilling strips into ⅜-inch Loose (Closed) Coils; eight 4-inch pieces of light turquoise quilling strips into ¼-inch Loose (Closed) Coils; and six 12-inch pieces of dark turquoise quilling strips into ½-inch Loose (Closed) Coils.

Adhere quilled circles randomly to night-light shade.

Tie sheer green pin-dot ribbon in a 2-inch bow; notch ends of streamers. Adhere bow to ribbon at bottom of shade as shown.

Sources: Night light from Darice; Style-a-Bility ribbon with sequins from Horizon Group USA; Fabri-Tac permanent adhesive from Beacon Adhesives Inc.

Floral Trinket Box

Design by **Sandy L. Rollinger**

Materials

Textured pale
  yellow card stock
⅛-inch-wide
  quilling paper
  strips: pink,
  bright green
Wooden recipe box
Craft paints: pink,
  light green, dark
  green
Small clear or
  amber flat-back
  beads
Flower paper
  punches: ⅝-inch,
  1-inch
Sandpaper
½-inch-wide soft
  paintbrush
Slotted quilling tool
Tweezers
Instant-dry paper
  glue

Project notes:
*Refer to Shape
Gallery, pages 5–7,
throughout to form
quilled shapes. Refer
to photo throughout
for placement.*

Sand and paint box. ***Note:*** *On sample project, lid sides are painted dark green; outer surface of lid top is painted light green; all other surfaces, including inset in lid and box interior, are painted pink. If your box has no inset in the lid, paint a light green border around the edges of the lid and paint center pink.*

Quilled Shapes

Vines: Cut eight 2½-inch pieces from bright green quilling strips. Form each into a Loose (Open) Scroll.

Leaves: Cut 16 (3-inch) pieces from bright green quilling strips. Form each into a Teardrop.

Hearts: Cut four 4-inch pieces from pink quilling strips. Form each into a Heart Scroll.

Finishing & Assembly

Punch four ⅝-inch flowers and two 1-inch flowers from textured pale yellow card stock. Adhere smaller flowers to corners of lid top.

Arrange and adhere two quilled leaves at each corner as shown, one on each side of punched flower. Center and adhere a heart on each short side of box lid.

On each long side of box lid, arrange and adhere a heart, two vines and two leaves as shown.

Adhere a bead centered atop each small flower and in the open space in each heart.

Arrange and adhere four leaves, broad ends facing, in center of inset, leaving an open space in the center. Arrange and adhere four vines as shown.

Adhere larger punched flowers to each other, alternating positions of petals; center and adhere to Teardrop leaves.

Adhere a bead to center of flower. Arrange and adhere three beads along each vine as shown.

Sources: *Clear Lustre Gems beads from Darice; Zip Dry Paper Glue from Beacon Adhesives Inc.*

Floral Frame

Design by **Sandy L. Rollinger**

Pour a small puddle of each color of paint onto disposable plate. Sponge paints onto frame; let dry.

Punch eight 1-inch flowers from medium blue card stock and eight ⅝-inch flowers from yellow card stock; set aside.

Quilled Shapes

Leaves: Cut 16 (4-inch) pieces from bright green quilling strips. Form each into a Teardrop.

Cut eight 4-inch pieces from bright green quilling strips. Form each into a V Scroll.

Dark blue flowers: Cut four 8-inch pieces from dark blue quilling strips. Form each into a Triangle, indenting broad base slightly for top edge of flower.

Finishing & Assembly

Beginning at the top and working down the sides, arrange quilled shapes and adhere to mat board as shown.

Pinch straight portions of each V Scroll together and adhere for stem. Position the sharp point of each quilled flower in the top of the stem, between coiled leaves. Center and adhere a yellow punched flower atop each stem.

Arrange Teardrop leaves in pairs with bases facing; center and adhere a punched blue flower atop each leaf pair.

When all punched and quilled components have been adhered to frame, center and adhere a silver bead to each blue punched flower and a clear bead to each yellow punched flower. Center and adhere a clear bead to the mat board at the top of each dark blue quilled flower.

Sources: Silver beads from The Robins Nest; Clear Lustre Gems clear beads from Darice; Zip Dry Paper Glue from Beacon Adhesives Inc.

Materials

Card stock: medium blue, yellow

⅛-inch-wide quilling paper strips: bright green, dark blue

8 x 10-inch white photo mat board with 4½ x 6½-inch oval opening

Wooden frame for 8 x 10-inch photo

Craft paint: medium blue, light blue, white

Small flat-back beads: silver, clear

Flower paper punches: ⅝-inch, 1-inch

Small kitchen sponge

Disposable plate

Slotted quilling tool

Tweezers

Instant-dry paper glue

Project notes:

Refer to Shape Gallery, pages 5–7, throughout to form quilled shapes. Refer to photo throughout for placement.

Materials

Printed paper:
  cream or off-
  white, pale green
White vellum
Complementary
  parchment
⅛-inch-wide
  quilling paper
  strips: cream or
  off-white, pale
  green
8 x 6-inch papier-
  mâché lidded
  box with photo
  window in lid
Cream craft paint

Wedding Memories Box

Design by **Sandy L. Rollinger**

Box

  Paint box inside and out; let dry and add a second coat if needed.
Option: Instead of painting box's interior, cut pieces of cream or off-white paper to fit and adhere.

  Cut satin braid trim to fit around edge of box lid and bottom of box; brush ends with permanent adhesive to prevent fraying.

  Using permanent adhesive throughout, adhere braid trim to lid and box as shown, positioning seam at center front on lid, where it will be concealed by decorative button. Let dry for 10 minutes, then adhere decorative button to center front edge of lid as shown.

Quilled Shapes

Marquises: Cut 24 (4-inch) pieces from cream quilling strips; form each into a Marquise. Set aside.

Leaves: Cut eight 3-inch pieces from pale green quilling strips; form each into a Teardrop for leaf. Set aside.

Vines: Cut eight 2-inch pieces from pale green quilling strips; form each into a Loose (Open) Scroll for vine. Set aside.

Roses: Form two Rectangle Roses from cream printed paper. Set aside.

Finishing

Adhere Marquises around edges of opening in lid, leaving room at corners and between quilled shapes to adhere pearls. Using tweezers, adhere pearls around opening as shown.

Punch six leaves from pale green printed paper. Emboss veins using stylus; snip edges using sharp scissors.

Arrange and adhere a rose and three punched, embossed leaves in lower left corner of lid and remaining leaves and rose in upper right corner as shown.

Arrange and adhere two quilled vines coming from each side of each rose. Arrange and adhere quilled leaves along vines; let dry.

Punch 10 flowers from cream printed paper and 10 flowers from vellum; indent centers using stylus. Adhere a vellum flower atop each cream flower, alternating positions of petals. Adhere a pearl in the center of each flower. Adhere flowers randomly to vines.

Hand-write using a calligraphy marker, or use computer to generate, sentiment on parchment to fit within an area 5 x 3½ inches. Trim to fit in opening in lid; insert in lid. *Option: Trim and insert photo into lid.*

Sources: FolkArt paint from Plaid Enterprises Inc.; Zip Dry Paper Glue and Fabri-Tac permanent adhesive from Beacon Adhesives Inc.

1½ yards ¼-inch-wide cream satin braid trim

35 (4mm) white pearls

Decorative gold shank button

Punches: ⅝-inch flower, 1-inch leaf

½-inch-wide flat paintbrush or foam brush

Craft knife

Stylus

Slotted quilling tool

Tweezers

⅛-inch hole punch

Glue: Instant-dry paper glue, permanent adhesive

Calligraphy pen

Computer and printer or photo to fit in lid (optional)

Project notes:

Refer to Shape Gallery, pages 5–7, throughout to form quilled shapes. Refer to photo throughout for placement. Adhere elements using fast-drying paper glue unless instructed otherwise.

Sunshine Frame

Design by **Mary Ayres**

Frame

Paint frame's back, side edges and edges of cutout opening yellow.

Cut a 7¾ x 3¾-inch rectangle from blue printed paper. Referring to Fig. 1, page 47, use circle template to lightly pencil a 2½-inch circle in center of paper, against the top edge. **Option:** *Trace around a glass of similar size.* Add increasingly larger circles around the first, spacing them unevenly and allowing them to run off the edges of the paper.

Using metallic gold sewing thread, machine-stitch over the penciled lines.

Lay stitched paper right side down; lay frame right side down on paper with top and side edges even. Trace around rounded upper corners and inner opening of frame; trim excess paper.

Using a dry sponge, rub blue ink over stitched lines and along edges of the printed paper. Adhere paper to top portion of frame.

Cut a 7¾ x 4¼-inch rectangle from striped printed paper; lay right side down. Lay frame right side down on paper with bottom and side edges even. Trace around rounded lower corners and inner opening of frame; trim excess paper. Adhere paper to lower portion of frame.

Adhere yellow fiber trim over seam between the printed papers, extending trim onto outer edges of frame and edges of center opening.

Adhere sheer yellow ribbon over corners of frame as shown, applying adhesive only to the ends of the ribbon on the frame edges.

Hand-print, or use a computer to generate, "SUNSHINE" on white card stock to fit in the bookplate. Trim card stock to fit; adhere it to back of bookplate. Thread bookplate onto blue ribbon; arrange bookplate and ribbon at an angle across bottom of frame, and adhere ribbon ends to frame sides.

Quilled Sun

Sun: Adhere three 24-inch pieces of yellow quilling strips end to end. Form into a 1¼-inch Loose (Closed) Coil. Adhere the coil to the frame at center top.

Rays: Cut 11 (6-inch) pieces of orange quilling strips; form each into ½-inch Loose (Closed) Coil, then shape into a Triangle. Arrange rays around sun and adhere to frame.

Sources: Frame from Provo Craft; Fresh Print printed papers from Déjà Views; Fabri-Tac permanent adhesive from Beacon Adhesives Inc.

Materials

White card stock
Printed paper:
  Banana Stripe,
  Tangerine Punch
⅛-inch-wide quilling
  paper strips:
  yellow, orange
7¾ x 8-inch flat
  wooden frame
Blue ink pad
Yellow craft paint
Black fine-tip
  marker
2¾ x ¾-inch copper
  bookplate
8 inches yellow
  fiber trim
Ribbon:
  10 inches
  ⅜-inch-wide blue
  jacquard stripe
  24 inches ½-inch-
  wide sheer yellow
  with white pin dots
Slotted quilling tool
Tweezers
Paintbrush
Small dry sponge
Circle templates
  (optional)
Sewing machine
  with metallic
  gold thread
Permanent adhesive
Computer and
  printer (optional)
Project notes:
*Refer to Shape
Gallery, pages 5–7,
throughout to form
quilled shapes. Refer
to photo throughout
for placement.
Adhere elements
using permanent
adhesive unless
instructed otherwise.*

Citrus Thanks
CONTINUED FROM PAGE 11

Quilled Citrus Thanks Card
Green Swirls

Berry Happy Birthday
CONTINUED FROM PAGE 13

Berry Happy Birthday Card
Strawberry Template

Baby Shower Invitation
CONTINUED FROM PAGE 15

Shower Invitation
Leaf

Party Favor Purses
CONTINUED FROM PAGE 25

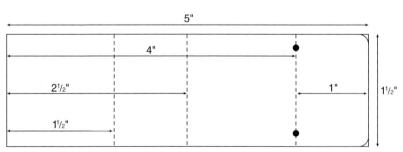

Party Favor Purses
Paper Purse

Birthday Gift Set
CONTINUED FROM PAGE 27

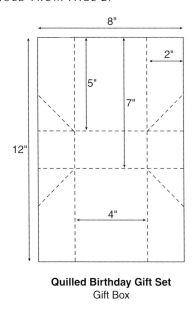

Quilled Birthday Gift Set
Gift Box

Floral Gift Bag
CONTINUED FROM PAGE 32

Floral Gift Bag
Flower

Sunshine Frame
CONTINUED FROM PAGE 45

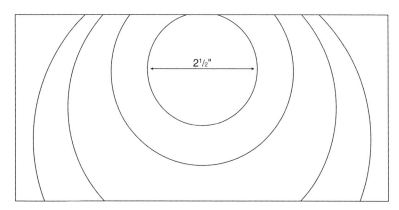

Fig. 1

Buyer's Guide

Check with your local retail store for product availability. If you can't find a product, contact the manufacturer directly to find a shop in your area.

Beacon Adhesives Inc.
(914) 699-3405
www.beaconcreates.com

Darice
(866) 432-7423
www.darice.com

Déjà Views
(860) 243-0303
www.dejaviews.com

Die Cuts With A View
(801) 224-6766
www.diecutswithaview.com

Dover Publications
www.doverpublications.com

EK Success Ltd.
www.eksuccess.com

Fiskars
(866) 348-5661
www.fiskarscrafts.com

Horizon Group USA
(800) 651-0616
www.horizongroupusa.com

K&Company
(888) 244-2083
www.kandcompany.com

Lake City Craft Company
(417) 725-8444
www.lakecitycraft.com

Lasting Impressions for Paper Inc.
(800) 9-EMBOSS (936-2677)
www.lastingimpressions.com

Paper Source
(888) PAPER-11 (727-3711)
www.paper-source.com

Plaid Enterprises Inc./ All Night Media
(800) 842-4197
www.plaidonline.com

Provo Craft/Coluzzle
mail-order source:
Creative Express
(800) 937-7686
www.provocraft.com

Quilled Creations Inc.
(877) 784-5533
www.quilledcreations.com

Ranger Industries Inc.
(732) 389-3535
www.rangerink.com

The Robins Nest
(435) 789-5387
www.robinsnest-scrap.com

Rubber Soul
(360) 779-7757
http://rubbersoul.myshopify.com

SEI
(800) 333-3279
www.shopsei.com

Stampin' Up!
(800) STAMP-UP (782-6787)
www.stampinup.com

Tsukineko Inc.
(425) 883-7733
www.tsukineko.com

We R Memory Keepers
(801) PICK-WER (742-5937)
www.wermemorykeepers.com

Whimsiquills
(877) 488-0894
www.whimsiquills.com